MIA HAMM

DISCOVER THE LIFE OF A SPORTS STAR

David and Patricia Armentrout

www.rourkepublishing.com

PHOTO CREDITS: All photos © Getty Images

Title page: *Mia in action during a Freedom vs. Courage game*

Editor: Frank Sloan

Cover and interior design by Nicola Stratford

Library of Congress Cataloging-in-Publication Data

Armentrout, David, 1962-
  Mia Hamm / David and Patricia Armentrout.
     v. cm. — (Discover the life of a sports star)
Includes bibliographical references (p.   ) and index.
Contents: The perfect sport — All American — College soccer — Team USA -- Olympic gold — Honors and awards — Mia Hamm Foundation — Mia's legacy.
  ISBN 1-58952-652-X (hardcover)
 1. Hamm, Mia, 1972—Juvenile literature. 2. Soccer players—United States—Biography—Juvenile literature. 3. Women soccer players—United States—Biography—Juvenile literature. [1. Hamm, Mia, 1972- 2. Soccer players. 3. Women—Biography.] I. Armentrout, Patricia, 1960- II. Title. II. Series: Armentrout, David, 1962- Discover the life of a sports star.
  GV942.7.H27A76 2003
  796.334'092--dc21

                            2003005932

Printed in the USA

CG/CG

Table of Contents

Mia stretches before a game with the Carolina Courage.

Mia Hamm

Mia Hamm is one of the most recognized female soccer players in the world. In fact, Mia is a record-breaking soccer star. Many consider Mia to be the world's best female soccer player.

Full Name:
Mariel Margaret Hamm
Teams:
• U.S. Women's National Team
• Washington Freedom WUSA
Position: Forward
Number: 9
Record: Ended 2002 as the world's all-time leading scorer with 136 career goals

The Perfect Sport

Mia was born March 17, 1972 in Selma, Alabama. Her parents, Bill and Stephanie, introduced Mia to soccer at a very early age. Soccer turned out to be the perfect sport for Mia.

Mia joined her first soccer team at the age of five, while living in Wichita Falls, Texas. Mia was young and small, but she could already **dribble** and move around opposing players with great speed and accuracy.

Mia plays for the U.S. Women's National team and the WUSA's Washington Freedom.

Mia, number 18, dribbles downfield during an Olympic Festival game.

All American

Mia's soccer skills only got better as she reached her teens. She played on school teams in Wichita Falls, and later in Burke, Virginia. Mia was named All American, which meant she was one of the best soccer players in the country.

In 1987, when Mia was just 15, she joined the U.S. National Team. Mia was the youngest woman ever to play for the national team.

Mia controls the ball in a Carolina Tar Heels game.

College Soccer

Mia won a sports **scholarship** to the University of North Carolina (UNC). Mia helped her team, the Tar Heels, win four **NCAA** national championships. Mia was named NCAA All American in 1990, 1992, and 1993. Mia ended her college soccer career as the Atlantic Coast Conference's all-time leading scorer with 103 goals, 72 **assists**, and 278 **points**.

Mia acknowledges her fans as she raises her 1995 MVP trophy.

Team USA

National teams around the world compete every four years for the World Cup. In 1991, Mia took a year off from college to play on the U.S. Team. The team won the first ever Women's World Cup that year. In 1995, the team placed third, and Mia was voted Most Valuable Player (MVP). In 1999, the United States hosted the third Women's World Cup. Mia helped her team make it to the final game, and they won the World Cup.

Olympic Gold

Women's soccer became a regular Olympic Event at the 1996 Summer Games. Team USA trained long and hard for the event. They were determined to show America what women's soccer was all about.

Mia scored a goal in the first round of the games and helped her team move on to the finals. Team USA played the final game against China in front of 76,000 fans and won the gold medal.

Mia races for the ball with Cecilia Sandell of Team Sweden during the 1996 Olympic Games.

Honors and Awards

Mia has proven to be a star player for the national team, but Mia also plays for the Washington Freedom. The Freedom is part of a new women's professional soccer league. Mia's skill, hard work, and determination have won her many honors and awards. For example, the **FIFA** has named Mia the Women's World Player of the Year for 2001 and 2002.

Ronaldo of Brazil and Mia Hamm of the United States with their trophies after winning the 2002 FIFA World Player Awards

Mia spends a day in New York City

Mia Hamm Foundation

Mia started the Mia Hamm Foundation in 1999. With the support of partners like Nike and Gatorade, the foundation raises funds for two causes. The first is bone marrow disease research. Mia's older brother Garret died of a bone marrow disease in 1997. Mia feels strongly about helping others with the disease. The foundation also supports programs for female athletes.

Mia's Legacy

Mia gets plenty of support and encouragement from family and friends. She gives back a winning attitude, especially to her teammates and fans.

Mia hopes to leave a positive and lasting legacy. With her book, *Go for the Goal: A Champion's Guide to Winning in Soccer and Life*, Mia will continue to be a positive role model and inspiration to athletes around the world.

Soccer fans wait patiently for Mia's autograph.

Dates to Remember

1972   Born March 17 in Selma, Alabama

1987   Joined the U.S. Women's National Team

1989   Attended UNC and played for the
        Tar Heels

1990   Made first international goal July 25
        against Norway

1994   Named U.S. Soccer's Chevrolet Female
        Athlete of the Year five years in a row
        from 1994-1998

1996   Member of the U.S. Olympic Gold
        Medal team

1999   Broke the all-time international scoring
        record, for men and women, against
        Brazil with her 108th career goal

2001   Became a founding player of the WUSA
        Washington Freedom

Glossary

assists (uh SISTS) — when a player passes the ball to another player who scores a goal

dribble (DRIB uhl) — controlling the ball on the ground with the feet

FIFA — Fédération International de Football Associations — Soccer's international governing body

NCAA — National Collegiate Athletic Association—regulates the conduct of intercollegiate athletic competition in the United States

points (POINTS) — a way to measure a player's attempt to score. A player gets two points for a goal and one point for an assist

scholarship (SKOL ur ship) — prize money used to pay for a college education

Index

Further Reading

Kirkpatrick, Rob. *Mia Hamm: Soccer Star*. Rosen Publishing Group, 2001
Latimer, Clay. *Mia Hamm*. Capstone Press, 2001
Rutledge, Rachel. *Mia Hamm: Striking Superstar*. The Millbrook Press, Inc. 2000

Websites To Visit

www.ussoccer.com
www.miafoundation.org/
www.wusa.com/
www.washingtonfreedom.com

About The Authors

David and Patricia Armentrout have written many nonfiction books for young readers. They have had several books published for primary school reading. The Armentrouts live in Cincinnati, Ohio, with their two children.